SOUL AND SILT

B. N. Helena

CONTENTS

Part I. Elements 1

    Shelf Break 3

    Paradigms 6

    Circular Fire 8

    Queen 9

Part II. Exile 11

    Mine 13

    Shark 15

    The Wind Is Fierce Tonight 17

    Trapped 18

Part III. Union 19

    Prayer I 21

    Prayer II 22

    Raven 23

    Toward Communion 25

PART I. ELEMENTS

Shelf Break[1]

Far beneath
the water's level surface,
the sea floor dives
down—a sudden,
hidden threshold,
a threat submerged but real,
the silent rift as land
abruptly ends
and another world begins.

Beyond a landlocked
cliff, where every grain
of rock seems known,
nothing lurks unseen,
and land though steep
continues, here an
inner vertigo
reveals a separateness,
a terror, a longing.

Alongside paved paths;
polite interactions;
trimmed trees;
clear, comforting margins
reign ceaseless, shifting
currents carrying swarms
of life and savage death
through mapless layers of deepening
darkness, upwelling, downwelling,

---

[1] The shelf break is the point at which the continental shelf (the floor of a shelf sea) ends and slopes steeply downward toward the abyssal plain.

a wilderness of swirling,
schooling fish diving,
darting, dazzling, rising;
scattering krill and thresher
shark; sea urchin crowning
the crawling carrier crab,
cardinalfish sauntering
around its stinging spines;
spinner dolphins leaping;

long-lived bowheads and humpbacks
breaching; anemonefish
sheltering in coral reefs;
red-fluorescing sand stargazers
signaling; pilot whales
whistling; tube anemones tugged
by distant tides; deep-sea
anglers hiding, luring,
lit only from within.

We dive blind,
seek ground,
gripping seamount flanks
for rest, evading rich
trenches, eroding
the rocks with our inquiry,
forcing the jagged rocks
to scar our flesh,
to let us see the truth,

to let us understand,
until the darkness yields
dense sediment—silent
sacrificial remains—
revealing then the basalt
bed, the abyssal altars'
echoing, fire-forged oracle
ever renewing in the slow
recycling of earth,[2]

until the depths are drained
and drenched in sunlight scouring
soul and silt, all lines
laid bare, every particle
purified, every cell
sanctified in stillness
as the molten mantle
rests, the core calms,
and sun illumines all.

Again beside the foamy
fringes of waves' reach,
children playing, gulls
gathering, salt breeze
bellowing, we breathe and grip
the glittering, shell-encrusted,
solid sand as currents
continue, real and full
though faint.

---

[2] The sea floor continuously forms from magma rising at mid-oceanic ridges, spreads slowly away from these volcanic centers, and dissolves back into the mantle at subduction zones under continental or oceanic crust.

Paradigms

I
Leaves unfurl,
revealing varying shades.

Diamond facets sparkle,
dispersing light's fire.

Perennials bloom,
each blossoming flower singular.

Sinuous tree branches
ascend a straight path,

their rustling leaves the wind's voice,
the leaves' voice the wind.

II
Words inflect,
filtering meaning through shifting
forms—

each shared thought
filled by others

(as when case reveals aspect
or verb class accords
with category of noun)

and no word as
simple as its surface
seems

(in the space under sound,
the infinite stumbles,
its brilliance seen)

as vanished sounds
surface, submerge, leave traces,
collide—cooled embers of thought
and time.

III
Identities unfold,
interacting with light and shadow,

shouldering lies
and longing's layers to ascertain
truth—

the unseen eternal
in the fragile, brutal ephemeral.

Listening to a like wave,
we (separate in time) speak
the same word,

follow the same inflections
though they've shifted slowly
like shorelines

and lives proceeding from a
steadfast root

through thickets

we strain to decipher
to find

the real beyond the word,
grace beyond grammar.

Circular Fire

Red and golden leaves,
long and thin,
rest gathered upright
in the clear glass jar
like twisting flames of sculpted
fire, tips scaling the rim,
motionless, eternal,
ethereal, earthen.

Unseen, the circular wall
surrounds the raging blaze,
shaping and guarding its glow.

Unheard, heedless, the flames
roar, creating, destroying,
yearning to be free.

Queen[3]

No need for the monarch's
mundane migration—

seeking solace—or renewal—
in austerity
far from native lands,

flying toward reflections—
such wide, high windows offered infinity—
seeking the Sun,

brilliant orange flutter
against bare grey, perchless walls,
brushfooted, solitary wanderer
wanting

escape from barren terrain,
bitter betrayals,
the prevailing harsh blandness,
fleeing even

sweetness of fragrant flowers
to find—
death or rebirth—

this flutter is force,
endurance, not whimsy,
safety's straightest course—

a second chrysalis—

---

[3] The queen butterfly (*Danaus gilippus*) is in the same genus as the monarch butterfly known for its annual migrations.

and lulls a deadly
distant storm—

spun from sadness,
secret yearning,
imagined meadows,
thoughts of companions,
the elusive, beloved source—

crafting stronger, clearer wings
to feed on nectar in the clouds'
store of vapor and light.

PART II. EXILE

Mine

See the metallic globes[4] on clear
glass shelves—incongruous, like stolen

sculpted deities in drab dress
ground down to sate a newer god

of greed and waste—precious dust–packed
gleaming husks of a sacred source

(if one could hear or see it)—or like
scattered, forgotten, brilliant beads

of a sea bride's bracelet, encased in reverent
earth, now traded for vows of wealth—

grey, glistening organs ripped
from living earth, their latent treasure

trembling, ghostlike already, longing
for water's weight, for the steady flow

of sustaining light through listening stillness,
the sponge's breath, the cold current's

communion, the sea anemone's
seductive sway—to lie on solid

molten sand, displaced from living
purpose etched through millions of years—

---

[4] Mining of polymetallic nodules, small metal concretions lying on the deep sea
floor, threatens to disrupt or eradicate richly diverse ecosystems about which little
is known. The nodules grow at a rate of about a millimeter per million years.

or like the severed sinewy claws
of a giant whose vanished foothold sent

the sea to overrun the earth.

Hear the silent screams against
the shattering strike—the seeker's own

exile—eternal distance—the need
for similes—irrevocable

loss—an empty looking glass.

Shark

He drank wine
at dinner—his face
puffed, his eyes
slouched, his body
drooped, his glasses
slipped down to his neck.

He threw wine
at walls—it flowed
from bottles shattering
with rage, ciphers
flung from a furious,
saddened, immovable core.

Wringing the sand of his past,
he wept. In the sun
his skin turned lobster
red. Distant but
parallel to shore—
safe from the rip

tides—fast, straight,
and strong he swam,
solitary and free.

Fierce and seductive
currents pulled
his thoughts to the horizon—
new lives, new smiles,
the threat behind joy—
as he drank the wine-dark

waves that lulled
exhaustion, embracing
spans of unseen
certainty, searching for grace,
releasing his terror at last,
innocent and bloody.

The Wind Is Fierce Tonight[5]

The wind is fierce tonight,
tossing white-tipped waves.
I don't fear Norse warbands
coursing on calm seas.

---

[5] Translation of the Old Irish poem *Is acher in gaíth innocht.* For the Irish text, see W. Stokes and J. Strachan, eds., *Thesaurus Palaeohibernicus ii* (Cambridge University Press, 1903), 290.

Trapped[6]

Her gaze has grown so weary
from going past the bars
that it takes in nothing else.
To her there are a thousand
bars—behind the bars,
pure nothingness.

Her smooth, strong step's
soft gait circling
the smallest space
is like a dance of force
that stuns a mighty
power at its base.

Sometimes her pupils
open noiselessly
to let an image pierce
her tensed-up, silent limbs,
to let it reach her heart
and disappear.

---

[6] Translation of "Der Panther" by Rainer Maria Rilke. For the German text, see
Rainer Maria Rilke, *Gesammelte Werke* (Anaconda Verlag, 2013), 436.

PART III. UNION

Prayer I

I wait for sunshine
shimmering on water,
warming my shoulders,
silently opening
a palace within.

Prayer II

Window and streaming light,
source and end,
dissolve the distance,
separation's lie,
the screeching stillness,
the silent cries.

Crashing waves,
buoy the sinking soul
that sought through lives
evolving—end
unknown—a union
to redeem and sanctify.

Sun and ray,
reveal the reason
for elements' joining and shattering;
guide a way
for longing's release as light
streams through transcendent source.

Raven

soothsayer,
scavenger,
sage common stranger

treetop sentinel,
sky roamer
alighting on litter
and nectar alike

at home everywhere,
everywhere hiding your power

you plucked the sun from your strivings,
the moon from your wanderings,
the wistful stars from your dream-born certainties

you summoned the clouds from your longing,
the lavish fires from your love-filled fury,
the peaceful, raging waters from your moody musing

you swung them up
to sky and earth
to comfort you, scold you,
inspire you, surround you,
never leave your side

spirit ally,
soul guide,
seeming shadow

you shelter me in
sudden sanctuary—
eternal, life-filled stillness—
extending your wings in flight
to soar above me

momentary peace

embracing your brethren,
you banish unkindness

solitary, strong,
you extinguish aloneness

leader of light and darkness,
dauntless you fly up

a constant cacophony
of concrete life
lifts in a conspiracy
of silence

Toward Communion

Flower-laden trees line
the silvery street.

Sky-flung petals fall to
soften our tread

over trapped,
twisting roots.

Distant voices fade, stilled
by silence

as sweet dogwood fragrance
lingers,

as golden-crowned kinglets
nest in festive branches
of forest.